The History of Zero

Exploring Our Place-Value Number System

Tika Downey

PowerMath™

The Rosen Publishing Group's
PowerKids Press™
New York

Published in 2004 by The Rosen Publishing Group, Inc.
29 East 21st Street, New York, NY 10010

Book Design: Ron A. Churley

Photo Credits: Cover, pp. 26–27 © Archivo Iconografico, S.A./Corbis; pp. 6–7 © Alan Schein
Photography/Corbis; p. 7 (top inset, bottom inset) © Joseph Sohm; Vision of America/Corbis; p. 7 (middle
inset) © Reuters NewMedia Inc./Corbis; pp. 8, 10 © Gianni Dagli Orti/Corbis; p. 12 © Araldo de Luca/Corbis;
p. 15 © David Lees/Corbis; p. 23 © Historical Picture Archive/Corbis; p. 25 © Artephot/Corbis; p. 29 ©
William James Warren/Corbis; p. 30 © Firefly Productions/Corbis.

Library of Congress Cataloging-in-Publication Data

Downey, Tika.
  The history of zero : exploring our place-value number system / Tika
Downey.
       v. cm. — (PowerMath)
Contents: It's nothing — Early counting systems — The first zero —
Zero is forgotten — Zero is invented again — Another zero — Zero in
the modern world.
  ISBN 0-8239-8982-8 (lib. bdg.)
  ISBN 0-8239-8869-4 (pbk.)
  6-pack ISBN: 0-8239-7377-8
  1. Zero (The number)—Juvenile literature. [1. Zero (The number) 2.
Number systems.] I. Title. II. Series.
  QA141.3 .D65 2004
  513—dc21
                              2002155344

Manufactured in the United States of America

Contents

It's Nothing

Zero—or 0—is one of our most basic math ideas. It is such a familiar idea that we have many different ways to say it. In addition to the word "zero," we use words like "none," "nada," "zilch," and "zip" when we want to say that there is nothing.

Zero plays a very important part in our place-value number system. In this system, the value of a **digit** (0, 1, 2, 3, 4, 5, 6, 7, 8, or 9) depends on where it is in the number. For example, in a 4-digit number, the digit in the farthest place to the right occupies the ones place. The next place to the left is the tens place. Then comes the hundreds place, then the thousands place, and so on for even larger numbers.

thousands
hundreds
tens
ones

4,321

Zero has had many different names over the centuries. Some of these names are shown on page 5.

Name for Zero or Nothing	Who Used It and When
sunya	Means "empty"; used in India around 400 A.D. to indicate an empty column on a counting board.
nulla	Latin word for "nothing"; used by a monk in Rome, Italy, around 825 A.D.
sifr	The Arab word based on the Indian word *sunya*. First used around 825 A.D.
kha	Arab word first used around 825 A.D. to mean "place" in a place-value number system. Later sometimes used to mean "zero."
nought, or naught, or aught	Old English words for "nothing." In use before 1150.
galgal	Means "zero"; first used around 1150 by a rabbi who spent most of his life in Spain. He had read Arab math books.
zephirum	The Latin word based on the Arab word *sifr*. First used in 1202 by an Italian merchant.
cipher or cypher	An English word based on the Arab word *sifr*. First used between 1350 and 1400.
zero	An English word based on the Arab word *sifr*. First used in a book published in 1604.

As long as there is a digit in each place in a number, we can understand what the number means. Even two different numbers that have several of the same digits are easy to understand. For example, it's easy to tell the difference between 4,021 and 421 when we have zero to put in the hundreds place of the larger number. Without zero, it would be confusing. Both numbers would be written the same way: | 4 | 2 | 1 |

We could leave an extra space between the 4 and the 2 in the larger number to show that 4 is in the thousands place, not the hundreds place: | 4 | | 2 | 1 |

However, everyone might not realize that the extra space was there, and they might think we meant 421, not 4,021.

Without 0, a $1.00 bill, a $10.00 bill, and a $100.00 bill would look almost the same. All of them would seem to have the same value—$1.00. They would all have just a 1 on them, with no zeros after it.

As this example shows, zero is a very important placeholder in a place-value number system. For thousands of years, however, people around the world used counting systems that did not include zero. Let's take a look at the history of numbers to find out when zero was invented and who invented it.

dusis. dipondi. tressis. quadra
sis. quinquis. sexis. Septisis.
octusis. et c e ꝫ e ꝛa.

Early Counting Systems

People began counting things long before they created a writing system or a number system. Early hunters cut a mark into a stick or animal bone for each animal they killed. These sticks or bones are known as **tally** sticks. Some of these tally sticks are 30,000 years old!

Other ancient people counted using their fingers, toes, elbows, knees, and other body parts. Still others counted by using pebbles or shells. One pebble or shell represented 1 animal killed, 1 sheep taken to the meadow to feed, or 1 of whatever was being counted. Yet another ancient counting system, used in many places around the world, used knotted strings.

None of these early counting systems had any need for zero. A person would not count zero animals killed or zero sheep taken to the meadow.

Many early counting systems, such as tally sticks and finger counting, continued to be used for centuries. The picture on page 8 comes from a book written in the 800s and explains a finger-counting system that was in use then.

9

100

1,000

4,000

10

Around 3500 B.C., Egyptians invented one of the world's first writing systems. Picture **symbols**, called **hieroglyphs**, represented words, ideas, and numbers. Short, straight lines were used for numbers 1 through 9. An upside-down "U" represented 10. One hundred was represented by a curled line, 1,000 by a lotus plant, 10,000 by a bent finger, 100,000 by a tadpole or frog, and 1,000,000 by a kneeling figure with raised arms.

The Egyptians did not need zero to write numbers, since they had special symbols for numbers such as 10, 100, 1,000, and 10,000. They also did not need zero as a placeholder, since they did not have a place-value system. It didn't matter if you wrote ꝋꝋ∩∩∩ or ∩∩∩ꝋꝋ. Both meant 230.

If the Egyptians wanted to represent 40, they wrote 4 symbols for 10. To represent 300,000, they showed 3 frogs or tadpoles. To represent 2,000,000, they showed 2 kneeling figures with raised arms.

11

The First Zero

The ancient **Babylonians** also had a writing system and a number system. The Babylonians ruled the area that is now southern Iraq from around 2300 B.C. until around 550 B.C. They used wedge-shaped symbols, called **cuneiform** (kyoo-NEE-uh-form), for their writing and numbers. There was a symbol for 1 and a symbol for 10. Babylonians formed all their numbers by combining these 2 symbols.

The Babylonians were the first people to use a place-value system. However, like the Egyptians, the Babylonians at first had no zero. There was no difference between the way they wrote 3,601 and the way they wrote 361. A person reading the written record had to figure out which number was meant by reading the words and sentences around the number.

Cuneiform writing was probably invented by the Sumerians about 1,000 years before the Babylonians began to use it. It may have been invented to help merchants keep records, but it was also used by doctors and government officials.

Later, the Babylonians tried leaving an empty space between the 6 and the 1 when they wrote 3,601. As we've already seen, that method didn't always work. Then someone had the idea to fill the empty space with a special mark that would act as a placeholder. The Babylonians had invented zero!

We don't know exactly when this happened. However, we do know from the clay tablets that still exist that Babylonians were using their zero by around 300 B.C. The Babylonian zero didn't look like our zero, but it was important because it was the first zero ever!

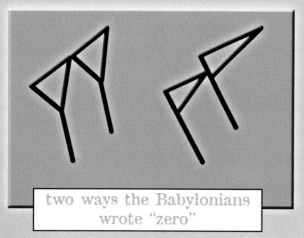

two ways the Babylonians wrote "zero"

Babylonians used a special tool to write on wet clay tablets. Then they hardened the tablets by baking them in the hot sun.

Zero Is Forgotten

You might think that after the Babylonians invented zero and a place-value system, everyone else would also use them. However, that's not what happened. Other ancient civilizations continued to use math without zero or a place-value system.

Greek math was concerned mainly with **geometry**. Since geometry measures lines, circles, rectangles, squares, and so forth, the Greeks did not need zero. For counting things, Greeks had a system very different from ours. Except for using a single line as the symbol for 1, they used the first letter of the word for a number as the symbol for that number. For example, "*pente*" was the Greek word for 5, so "p" was the symbol for 5. "*Deka*" was their word for 10, so "d" was the symbol for 10.

Like the Egyptians, the Romans did not need zero because they had special symbols for numbers like 10, 100, and 1,000.

Ancient Romans had 7 numerals in their system, which they used to form all of their numbers. For numbers consisting of more than 1 numeral, the usual rule was that you added the numerals together to find the value for the number. For example, III = 1 + 1 + 1 = 3, XV = 10 + 5 = 15, CC = 100 + 100 = 200, and so on. However, in a number such as IV, where the numeral on the left has a lower value than the numeral on the right, you subtracted the left numeral from the right one. So IV = 5 – 1 = 4. In the same way, IX = 10 – 1 = 9, XC = 100 – 10 = 90, and so on.

Roman number	our number
I	1
V	5
X	10
L	50
C	100
D	500
M	1,000

ancient Chinese numerals

○	│	‖	‖‖	‖‖‖	‖‖‖‖	⊤	⊤⊤	⊤⊤⊤	⊤⊤⊤⊤
0	1	2	3	4	5	6	7	8	9

○	—	=	≡	≣	☰	│	⊥	⊥	⊥
0	1	2	3	4	5	6	7	8	9

numbers written with Chinese numerals

⊤	≡	‖‖‖		⊤⊤	○	○	⊤	≡
6	5	4		7	0	0	6	4

Zero Is Invented Again

More than 800 years after the Babylonians invented zero and a place-value system, they were reinvented by **mathematicians** in India. Around 500 A.D., a **Hindu** mathematician named Aryabhata (ar-yuhb-HUT-uh) invented a place-value number system. Then around 650 A.D., zero appeared in Hindu math.

These Hindu math advances were important because they were not forgotten like the Babylonian inventions were. Instead, they spread throughout Asia and Europe. In fact, our zero and place-value number system come from the Hindu system!

These Hindu math ideas reached China by 800 A.D. At that time, Chinese mathematicians already used a place-value system, but their system had no zero. The Chinese adopted zero from the Hindu system and made it a part of their own. To represent zero, Chinese mathematicians drew a small circle.

The Chinese had more than one way to write numerals from 0 to 9. Two different systems are shown on page 18. When writing large numbers, the Chinese often combined numerals from the two different systems.

different forms of Hindu-Arabic numerals

1 2 3 4 5 6 7 8 9 0

١ ٢ ٣ ٤ ٥ ٦ ٧ ٨ ٩

١ ٢ ٣ ٤ ٥ ٦ ٧ ٨ ٩

١ ٢ ٣ ٤ ٥ ٦ ٧ ٨ ٩ ٠

١ ٢ ٣ ٤ ٥ ٦ ٧ ٨ ٩

١ ٢ ٣ ٤ ٥ ٦ ٧ ٨ ٩

Around this same time, Hindu ideas were being adopted in Arab lands. Arab mathematicians first learned about the Hindu number system from an Indian book on astronomy that was translated into Arabic around 800 A.D.

Twenty-five years later, a famous Arab mathematician named al-Khwarizmi (al–hwar-REEZ-me) wrote a book about Hindu numerals. Al-Khwarizmi's book helped to spread knowledge of the Hindu number system throughout the Arab world. Because Hindu numbers were made known to much of the world by Arab mathematicians, the numbers were commonly called Arabic numerals. Today the numbers are often called Hindu-Arabic numerals.

By 1000 A.D., the Hindu system had reached Spain, which was then part of the Arab world. However, Hindu ideas did not spread beyond Spain to other European countries for another 2 centuries.

Hindu-Arabic numerals were written in different ways in various parts of the Arab world. The forms also changed over time. Page 20 shows some of the different ways Hindu-Arabic numerals were written.

Around 1200 A.D., an Italian merchant's son named Leonardo Fibonacci (fih-buh-NAH-chee) often traveled in Arab lands in search of goods for his father's store. On these travels, he learned about the Hindu number system. Fibonacci recognized that the Hindu numerals had many advantages over the Roman numerals that were then used in Europe. The 4 basic math operations—addition, subtraction, multiplication, and division—could all be performed much more easily with Hindu numerals than with Roman numerals.

In 1202, Fibonacci wrote a book explaining the benefits of the Hindu number system. European mathematicians soon began to use Hindu numerals. However, most merchants and bankers were unwilling to change the way they had been doing things for centuries. They believed that it was too easy to change the written Hindu numerals and feared that some people would try to cheat others. Roman numerals continued to be used in most of Europe for more than 3 centuries after Fibonacci wrote his book.

This picture comes from a book printed in Germany around 1494. The number of the page, or *folium*, is written in Roman numerals in the upper right corner. It says "274."

De erpugnatiōne Cōstātinopolis

Another Zero

Around the same time that Hindu mathematicians were inventing zero and a place-value system, similar advances were being made on the other side of the world by the **Maya**. The Maya ruled the area that is now southern Mexico and Guatemala. Their civilization was at its most powerful between about 300 A.D. and 900 A.D.

The Maya invented their number system to help them create calendars that gave exact information. They had a sacred calendar so they would know when to have their religious ceremonies. They had a seasonal calendar so their farmers would know when to plant their crops. The Maya also had a third calendar that counted all the days since the world began.

This Mayan book, made around 1200, is a manuscript. That means it was written by hand. Four rows of circles with drawings inside them stretch across the lower part of the manuscript. These are the day signs for the days of the sacred calendar.

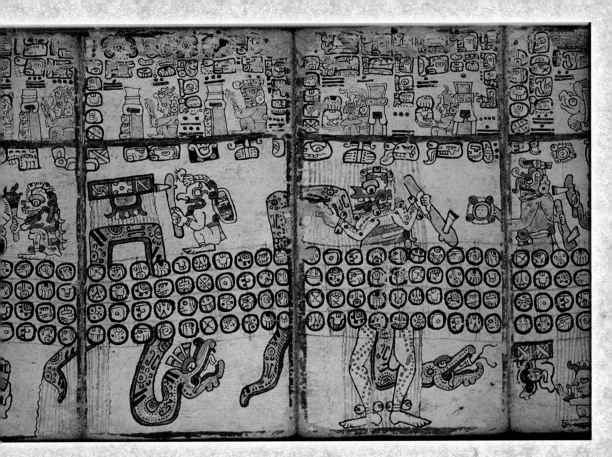

some Mayan day signs

 Imix = waterlily

 Chuen = frog

 Kan = corn

 Men = eagle

The Mayan number system had 3 symbols: a dot, a straight line, and a shell. The dot represented the number 1, the straight line represented the number 5, and the shell represented zero. The Maya made all their numbers by combining these symbols.

The Maya also had a place-value system, although their system was different from ours. Our numbers are written from left to right. In the Mayan system, the digits in multidigit numbers were written from top to bottom. We use the numbers 0, 1, 2, 3, 4, 5, 6, 7, 8, and 9 to create all our numbers larger than 9. The Maya used the numbers from 0 through 19 to create all their numbers larger than 19.

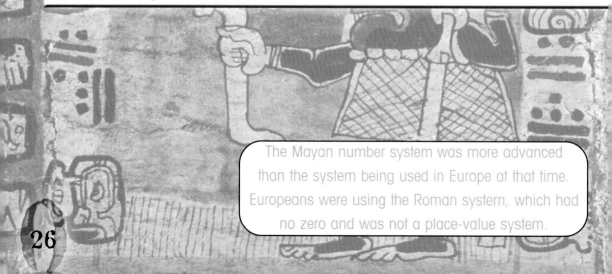

The Mayan number system was more advanced than the system being used in Europe at that time. Europeans were using the Roman system, which had no zero and was not a place-value system.

Mayan numbers

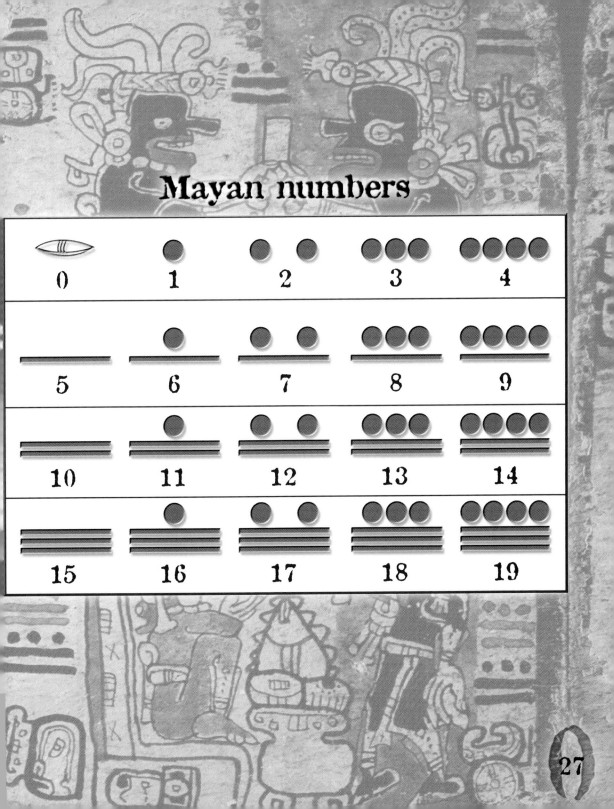

Zero in the Modern World

By the mid-1500s, the Hindu-Arabic number system had become accepted throughout Europe. It spread to the New World when Europeans began to establish colonies in North America in the late 1500s.

Today, zero is important around the world because of computers. Computers understand and record all information in **binary code**. Binary code is a number system built on two digits. The binary code in use today is built on the digits 1 and 0. Every letter of the alphabet and every Arabic numeral is represented in binary code by a series of ones and zeros. This is the language of computers.

In the United States, binary code uses 7 digits for each letter of the alphabet and each Arabic numeral.

letter	binary code
A	1000001
B	1000010
C	1000011
D	1000100
E	1000101

computer microchip

Arabic numeral	binary code
1	0110001
2	0110010
3	0110011
4	0110100
5	0110101

The ones and zeros of binary code don't mean what 1 and 0 mean in ordinary math. Inside a computer, there is a series of on-off switches. Binary code tells the computer which switches to turn on and which switches to turn off. In this language, 1 means "on" and 0 means "off."

Zero has made an astonishing journey over thousands of years. It didn't even exist in the earliest counting systems. The first zero ever invented was used only as a placeholder, but it had no meaning by itself. Over the centuries, the digit zero has changed and taken on new meanings. Today we live in a world that could not function without zero in our number systems.

digital **TV** control room

Glossary

Babylonian (ba-buh-LOH-nee-uhn) Someone who lived in the ancient kingdom of Babylonia, in what is now southern Iraq.

binary code (BY-nair-ee KOHD) The language of computers, which uses ones and zeros.

cuneiform (kyoo-NEE-uh-form) Having the shape of a wedge.

digit (DIHJ-it) Any of the figures 0, 1, 2, 3, 4, 5, 6, 7, 8, and 9.

geometry (gee-AHM-uh-tree) A type of math that measures and compares points, lines, angles, surfaces, and solid shapes.

hieroglyph (HY-ruh-gliff) One of the signs in a writing system that uses pictures instead of letters and words.

Hindu (HIN-doo) Someone who follows the religion of Hinduism.

mathematician (math-muh-TIH-shun) An expert in math.

Maya (MY-uh) An ancient Native American people who lived in southern Mexico or Guatemala and spoke a Mayan language.

symbol (SIM-buhl) Something that stands for something else.

tally (TA-lee) Something on which marks are made to keep count.

Index